D1647893

REMARKABLE
BIRDS

Thanks to the creative team:
Senior Editor: Alice Peebles
Fact checking: Kate Mitchell
Design: www.collaborate.agency

Hungry Tomato™
A division of Lerner Publishing Group, Inc.
241 First Avenue North
Minneapolis, MN 55401 USA

For reading levels and more information, look up
this title at www.lernerbooks.com.

Main body text set in Mate Regular 10/12.

Library of Congress Cataloging-in-Publication Data

The Cataloging-in-Publication Data for *Remarkable
Birds* is on file at the Library of Congress.
ISBN 978-1-5124-0626-9 (lib. bdg.)
ISBN 978-1-5124-1167-6 (pbk.)
ISBN 978-1-5124-0920-8 (EB pdf)

Manufactured in the United States of America
1-39299-21136-4/5/2016

ANIMAL BESTS

REMARKABLE BIRDS

BY JOHN FARNDON
ILLUSTRATED BY CRISTINA PORTOLANO

HUNGRY
TOMATO™

GOLDEN EAGLES LIKE TO MAKE
THEIR EYRIES HIGH UP ON
STEEP CLIFF FACES.

CONTENTS

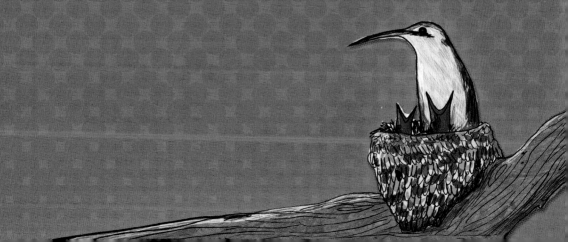

SMART BIRDS

If you ever get called "bird brain" you should take it as a compliment. Despite their small size, some birds are very, very clever indeed. And they have special skills and characteristics that help them to survive.

First, here's a taste of just how amazing birds are, before we even get on to the really clever stuff . . .

SAVANNA SPEEDSTERS

Although the fastest creature on land is the cheetah, which can reach 75 miles per hour (120 kilometers per hour), the supercharged ostrich (left) is not so far behind. It can't fly, but its giant legs whirl it along to nearly 60 miles per hour (100 km/h)!

BIG BIRDS

The ostrich is also the largest living bird. It grows up to 9 feet (2.7 meters) tall and can weigh more than 344 pounds (156 kilograms). But the ostrich is too heavy to fly. The largest flying bird is the wandering albatross (below). Its wings stretch out 11.6 feet (3.5 m). The heaviest flying birds are bustards.

THAT'S FLYING

The fastest flier is the peregrine falcon (right), which can reach astonishing speeds when stooping —diving on its prey with its wings tucked in. Some falcons have been recorded flying 242 miles per hour (389 km/h). But swifts are the fastest in level flight, with the white-throated needletail flashing along at 105 miles per hour (169 km/h).

WINGING IT

Terns are astonishing for their long flights. In fact, some almost never land. After leaving its nesting grounds as a youngster, the sooty tern (left) remains aloft for up to ten years, only landing on water from time to time. Scientists once recorded a common tern flying more than 16,000 miles (26,000 km) from Finland to Australia, covering 125 miles (200 km) every day.

OLD BIRDS

In 2014, a flamingo called Greater had to be put to sleep because it was suffering from rheumatism. Greater was eighty-three years old! Flamingoes (right) are not the only birds that can live into their eighties. Parrots and albatrosses can too. Cookie, a Major Mitchell's cockatoo in Chicago's Brookfield Zoo, was nearly eighty-three in 2016.

CLEVER!

Folktales often tell how crows and their relatives, the rooks, are clever tricksters. But scientists thought these were just stories—until they started doing experiments. Then they found that these birds are very clever. In fact, they're cleverer than most humans are by the age of seven! So don't try and trick a crow.

DINNER'S UP

Long ago, ancient Greek storyteller Aesop told a fable about a crow dropping stones into a narrow jug so that the water rose and it could drink. Scientists tested this story by putting a tempting worm on a cork at the bottom of a deep jar. Sure enough, all the rooks in the test dropped stones into the jar, raising the water level and getting the worm.

LET THAT BE A LESSON

To teach visitors the importance of looking after litter, staff at the Montecasino Bird Garden in Johannesburg, South Africa, tried an experiment. They trained crows to pick up litter and drop it in a garbage can. The crows proved very good at the job!

ROOKS RULE

Rooks and their relatives are very social birds. In winter, they often gather to roost (sleep) in large colonies in the treetops. These are known as rookeries.

THE TOOL FOR THE JOB

Most scientists think that using tools shows an animal is really clever. The crows of the Pacific islands of New Caledonia are perhaps the cleverest tool users of all. These crows don't just use a stick to get insects out of holes in trees. They first bend the end of the stick into a hook, so it works even better at poking out insects.

GETTING THE MESSAGE

Many animals have distinctive calls. But apart from humans and whales, birds are the only other animals that sing. A song is not a single sound, but a tune that goes up and down in a particular pattern, like music. Birds usually sing early in the morning. They sing to attract a mate or to declare their territory. Outside the tropics, it is mostly male birds that sing.

THE LARK RISING

The best singers are songbirds, such as warblers, sparrows, blackbirds, and robins. And the most loved songbird is the skylark (above). Other birds sing while perching, but the skylark soars up into the sky as it pours out a glorious, very complex blizzard of notes.

BOOM TIME

The bittern's call is not exactly beautiful. But it's certainly effective and often haunting to hear in the lonely marshes that are its home. The low, booming sound carries more than 3 miles (5 km) away on a still night.

ROOTS MUSIC

Male kakapos of New Zealand don't so much sing as blow their own trumpets. To attract a female, they inflate air sacs in their chest to make a long trumpeting sound, mixed in with high "chings." They cannot fly, so they dig a bowl-shape in the ground and sing from that.

SINGING DUELS

Marsh wrens don't always sing by themselves. Sometimes a male will engage in a singing duel with another male. This is isn't just a battle to see who can sing loudest. It's an elaborate duet. One bird takes the lead vocal line, and the other slots his tune in between.

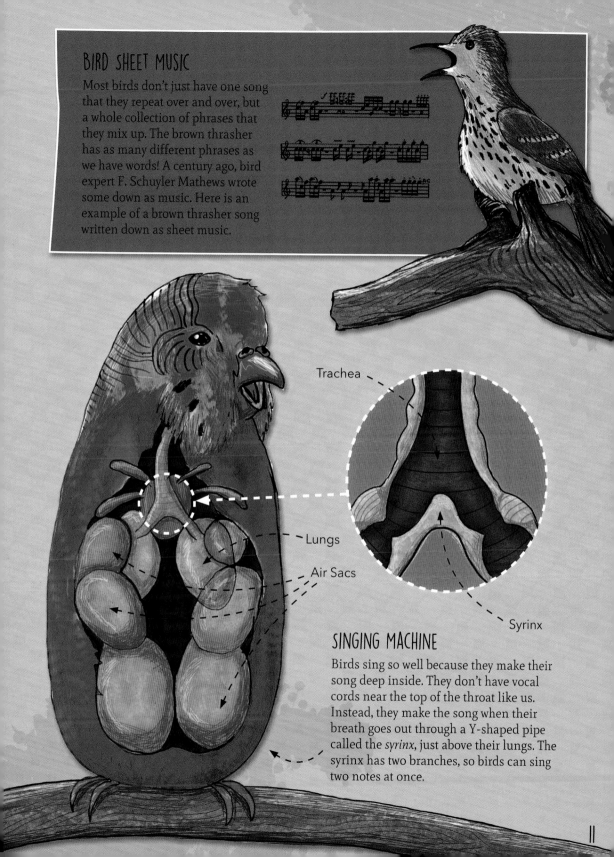

BIRD SHEET MUSIC

Most birds don't just have one song that they repeat over and over, but a whole collection of phrases that they mix up. The brown thrasher has as many different phrases as we have words! A century ago, bird expert F. Schuyler Mathews wrote some down as music. Here is an example of a brown thrasher song written down as sheet music.

Trachea

Lungs

Air Sacs

Syrinx

SINGING MACHINE

Birds sing so well because they make their song deep inside. They don't have vocal cords near the top of the throat like us. Instead, they make the song when their breath goes out through a Y-shaped pipe called the *syrinx*, just above their lungs. The syrinx has two branches, so birds can sing two notes at once.

DETECTOR POWER

Most birds rely on sharp eyesight to navigate and find food, but not oilbirds and swiftlets. They sleep in dark caves by day and fly only at night in dense forests. These birds have their very own super sense—an echolocation system as good as any bat's.

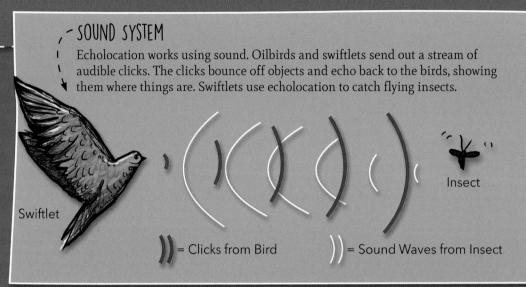

SOUND SYSTEM

Echolocation works using sound. Oilbirds and swiftlets send out a stream of audible clicks. The clicks bounce off objects and echo back to the birds, showing them where things are. Swiftlets use echolocation to catch flying insects.

Swiftlet

Insect

)) = Clicks from Bird   )) = Sound Waves from Insect

ECHO SENSE

Oilbirds live in northern South America and eat fruit. They have specially adapted eyes that help them to see well in twilight. This enables oilbirds to find food at dusk and dawn. But they use echolocation to find their way around the dark caves where they sleep during the day, and avoid bumping into each other!

OPEN WIDE

Like swiftlets, nightjars fly in the dark and catch insects by "hawking"—gulping them down in mid-air. But nightjars don't use echolocation. Instead their big eyes help them to see at dusk and dawn when they hunt—and their beak can open so wide they're much less likely to miss!

BIRD'S NEST SOUP

Just like the oilbird, the swiftlets of southern Asia and Indonesia sleep in caves and fly at night. They eat insects, not fruit, though. Their nests in caves are made mostly of their own gooey saliva. In China, people gather these nests by climbing long poles and cook the nests in water to make bird's nest soup.

GUACHÁRO CAVE

Oilbirds live in huge colonies, clinging to cave walls with tiny, hooklike feet. They got their name because long ago oilbird chicks were caught and boiled down to make oil. The most famous oilbird colony is in Guacháro Cave in Venezuela, home to more than fifteen thousand oilbirds. Their name is *guacháro* in Spanish.

I HEAR YOU

The real deadly assassins of the night are owls, and especially barn owls. When they go out hunting at night, they are looking for mice, voles, rats, and even rabbits. They find their prey in the dark with their amazing eyes and even more amazing hearing.

OWL FACE

Unlike many birds, an owl's eyes face forward. This means that both eyes work together to help the bird judge distance, as human eyes do. The special cone-like shape of each cheek focuses light and sound towards the owl's ears and eyes. Barn owls' eyes aren't quite as big as those of other species, but they are backed by their superb hearing.

BEHIND YOU!

An owl's eyes have a fairly narrow angle of vision. But this helps to keep their eyesight super-sharp. The owl can also see in any direction simply by turning its head. Its neck is so flexible it can rotate its head to face backward!

SUPER HEARING

A recent experiment by scientists with a
barn owl in a vast, completely dark room
showed the owl can pinpoint a mouse by
sound alone. Humans can work out direction because we have
two ears. This means that if a sound is not straight ahead, it
reaches one ear slightly earlier than the other ear. Barn owls
pinpoint sounds in the same way, but much better because their
hearing is so acute.

OFFSET EARS

A barn owl's earholes are
slightly offset – slightly
higher on one side than
the other. This means that
when they are flying along
face down, sounds reach
one ear marginally ahead of
the other. This is why their
directional sense of sound
is so accurate.

Right
Ear

Left
Ear

GHOSTLY WINGS

Some people find barn owls eery because they
fly silently on great, white, ghostly wings. But
any noise would alert their prey and disrupt the
precise hearing they need to track targets. Their
silent flight depends on special features in the
wings, such as soft, downy feathers that don't
rub together, and soft noise-damping
fringes on the wing tips.

SUPER SENSES

With high-tech cameras, we can see things clearly at great distances. But to the eagle, that comes naturally. It has the animal world's sharpest eyes. It can see clearly as far as 50 miles (80 km) away—five times further than humans can.

SHARP EYES

An eagle's huge eyes let in a lot of light. Their eyes are also five times more densely packed with receptors than humans—like a camera with mega pixels. The lens changes shape more quickly than ours, to keep things in focus. Even the fovea (the receptor structure at the center of each eye) is much deeper than human eyes, making eagle eyes like telephoto lenses. Eagles see more colors too!

HIGH HOMES

Eagles' nests are called eyries. Golden eagles like to make their eyries high up on steep cliff faces. That keeps their eggs entirely safe from most predators. But it means the only way out for the young chicks is to learn to fly straight away!

Eagle Vision   **Human Vision**

PANORAMIC VIEW

Because eagle's eyes are on the sides of the head, they can see almost all the way around, giving them a panoramic view. And yet, unlike most birds (apart from owls and other birds of prey), their eyes face partly forward so that the view from each one overlaps. The slightly different view from each eye enables eagles to judge distances, like humans. This is called binocular vision.

LIFTING POWER

An eagle doesn't have strong jaws like a big cat or wolf. But it has sharp talons and a razor-sharp beak that can be just as deadly for prey. Its talons are also amazingly strong. An eagle can grab a heavy victim in its talons and fly with it back to its nest. A golden eagle (weighing roughly 14 pounds (6 kg)) can carry a dog or even a small deer (roughly 80 pounds (36 kg)) in its talons.

EAGLE HUNTING

Golden eagles are the least tame animals you can imagine. Yet 2,000 years ago or more, Kazakh people learned to train these eagles to hunt red foxes. Training eagles takes many years. The Kazakhs call those who hunt with eagles *bürkitshi*, and most of these hunters now live in Mongolia.

17

VANISHING ACTS

Many birds are masters of the art of vanishing to avoid birds of prey. Their drab plumage provides the perfect camouflage when seen from above, blending almost invisibly into the surroundings. Birds that sleep or forage on the ground in the daytime, nesting females, and young chicks all need to be particularly well-camouflaged.

NOT STANDING OUT

Most birds rely on the colors and patterns in their feathers to avoid being seen. But the bittern uses another kind of camouflage. When it's among tall reeds, it sticks its neck and beak up high in the air so that it takes on the shape of the reeds. That makes it surprisingly hard to see from a distance. This is called "posture camouflage."

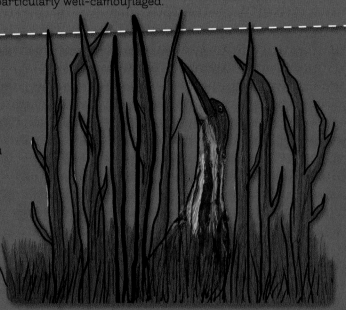

SNOW BLIND

To be effective, camouflage has to match a bird's surroundings. So the brown colors that suit forest birds are no good for Arctic birds, where dark colors would show up against the snow. That's why, unlike every other owl, the snowy owl has brilliant white plumage that makes it merge into the Arctic snow—not just for predators, but also for the owl's prey.

KEEPING QUIET

Mother birds are very vulnerable while they sit on the nest waiting for eggs to hatch. So most females have drab, mottled patterns to avoid being seen. Ground-nesting birds, such as ducks, are especially at risk. If a predator comes near, the mother duck will sit tight on her nest until the last minute, before exploding into the air to draw attention away from her eggs.

TAKING A LEAF

During the day, nightjars rest on the ground where they are open to attack, not just by birds of prey, but by four-legged hunters as well. So they need to be very well-camouflaged. They usually lie down amid leaf litter, where their indistinct brown coloring makes them really hard to see.

THE DISAPPEARING POTOO

Few birds are better at camouflage than the common potoo of Central and South America. It flies at night to hunt insects, like its close relative the nightjar. But during the day, it perches on tree stumps, and is disguised to look like part of the stump. If danger threatens, it freezes completely, looking just like a broken branch.

BRILLIANT BUILDERS

Some birds are great home builders. While many birds just lay their eggs in a hole on the ground, some construct nests. Each species has its own distinctive nest, from the neat cup of a blackbird to the sewn-up leaf of the tailorbird. But no birds have nests as elaborate as those of weaver birds.

After creating a ring, the weaver pulls the grass around the outside!

It leans back to pull the grass back through.

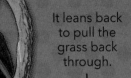

WEAVING A NEST

Weaver birds skillfully weave twigs together with their beaks to make sturdy nests. The master of them all is the baya weaver of India. Its nest is like a hanging basket. The male makes it from grass and the leaves of paddy rice, tying them all together with complex knots and stitches.

Then the bird folds the end and threads it through the ring.

The bird perches on the ring as it knots the grass.

DESIGNER NEST

Male satin bowerbirds of Australia make some of the flashiest nests of any bird. Their nests have roofs, which is why they are called bowers. The bird also puts brightly colored objects across the entrance to impress females—red flowers, blue stones, bits of colored plastic, and much more.

BIRD TOWN

Sociable weaver birds live in southern Africa and live up to their name. They construct a huge, intricate town of nests attached to trees and poles, the most spectacular structures built by any bird. Pairs of birds have their own nests within the town, but they all work together to create a home for one hundred or more pairs. Living together like this means that one of the birds can be on the lookout for danger.

ART OF THE NEST

Ruby-throated hummingbirds come from the south to spend the summer in eastern North America. They build beautiful little nests. The female starts by knotting spider silk round a tree branch to anchor it, and weaves together bark, leaf strands, and more silk to create a tiny cup Then she carefully lines it with fur or feathers for warmth. Finally, she decorates the outside with green lichen for camouflage.

TOOL USERS

Crows are not the only birds to use tools. In fact, many more birds can use tools than you might think, including woodpecker finches, vultures, nuthatches, and macaws. Birds can't hold tools in their hands, but their beaks do the trick.

EGG CRACKER

Ostrich eggs are so tough that the Egyptian vulture finds them hard to crack. So the vulture picks up a stone and flings it at the egg again and again until it smashes. Ravens are even cleverer, though. They give an egg to a vulture to smash. Then, when the vulture has done the hard work, the ravens pair up to drive off the vulture and take the egg themselves.

NUTCRACKERS

Nuts are hard to eat, even for a bird with a beak as tough as the hyacinth macaw. The nut slips away as the bird tries to bite it. So the clever macaw wraps chewed leaf around the nut to hold it in place, or even uses a makeshift clamp made of bits of wood.

GETTING UNDER THE BARK

Brown-headed nuthatches live in the pine forests of Louisiana. They're so small, it's easy to think they can't be that clever. But the little nuthatches have been seen using chisels made from flakes of bark. They chisel away with these at the bark of a tree to get at the insects underneath. The birds are not strong, though, so it only works where the bark is quite flaky.

WHO NEEDS A DRILL?

Woodpecker finches live on the Galapagos islands. They are not woodpeckers at all but, like woodpeckers, can dig out insects from trees. While woodpeckers drill a hole, woodpecker finches probe for insects with a cactus spine or twig. Recently, woodpecker finches found some blackberry twigs and stripped away all the thorns except a few at the end—a perfect barbed probe.

MARVELOUS MIMICS

Birds can make a wide range of sounds and be amazing mimics. The crow family, parrots, myna birds, bowerbirds, mockingbirds, and thrashers are the best at doing impressions. Older birds especially may have thousands of sounds.

ALEX (ANIMAL LEARNING EXPERIMENT)

Alex the African grey was a very famous talking parrot. He was trained to talk by animal psychologist Irene Pepperburg for more than thirty years. Before this experiment, scientists thought that birds could only mimic. But Alex learned more than one hundred words and seemed to understand them, putting them together in different ways.

KEY UNDERSTANDING

Pepperburg showed that Alex the parrot didn't just copy words but had some idea what they meant. For example, he always said "key" when he was shown a key—no matter what shape, size, or color it was. And if he was given a nut when he said, "I wanna banana," he'd sulk and ask for a banana again—sometimes even throwing the nut back to the researcher first!

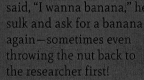

GOODBYE

Sadly, Alex the parrot died quite young, at just thirty-one years old in 2007. His last words to Pepperburg were, "You be good, see you tomorrow. I love you."

PARROT-FASHION

The best talking birds of all are parrots. There are countless tales of parrots and their way with words. People use the term "parrot-fashion" to describe mindless learning, though. The idea is that parrots can only mimic humans, without ever understanding words.

COPY CATS

The best bird mimics are the lyrebirds of Australia. They are famous for their spectacular tails and their astonishing vocal abilities. Usually they mimic the sounds of other birds, but those raised in captivity can mimic chainsaws, radios, camera shutters, car alarms, and other man-made sounds with startling accuracy.

MYNAH DETAILS

Mynah birds are small, black birds related to starlings. They are often kept as pets and astonish people with their ability to mimic human speech, learning many words and phrases. One mynah, known as Kaleo, formed a strong bond with a dog called Jack. After Jack died, Kaleo kept saying, "I love Jack," and asking where he was.

JOURNEY BIRDS

Birds make the most astonishing journeys of any animal. Some, such as the wandering albatross, are on the move all the time. But the most epic journeys are migrations, as birds fly to warmer regions to escape the winter, or return to places where there is more food in summer. The greatest annual migrations are made by waders and seabirds.

Alaska

New Zealand

THE FLIGHT RECORD

Each year wading birds called bar-tailed godwits migrate from Alaska to New Zealand. In 2007, a godwit was recorded flying 7,145 miles (11,500 km) from Alaska to New Zealand nonstop over the Pacific Ocean. That's the longest nonstop flight ever recorded. Amazingly, it took just nine days, so the little bird was flying nearly 800 miles (1,300 km) every day!

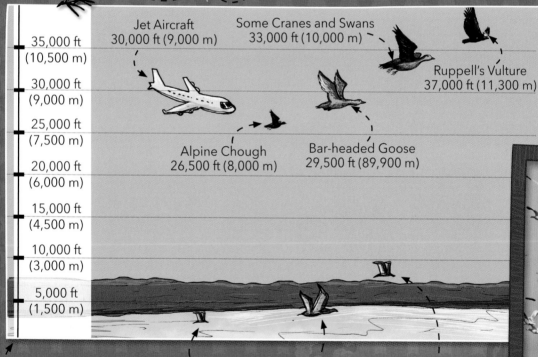

Altitude	
35,000 ft (10,500 m)	Jet Aircraft 30,000 ft (9,000 m)
	Some Cranes and Swans 33,000 ft (10,000 m)
30,000 ft (9,000 m)	Ruppell's Vulture 37,000 ft (11,300 m)
25,000 ft (7,500 m)	
20,000 ft (6,000 m)	Alpine Chough 26,500 ft (8,000 m)
	Bar-headed Goose 29,500 ft (89,900 m)
15,000 ft (4,500 m)	
10,000 ft (3,000 m)	
5,000 ft (1,500 m)	

Songbirds
4,000 ft (1,200 m)

Ducks and Geese
5,000 ft (1,500 m)

Bald Eagle
10,000 ft (3,000 m)

HIGH–FLIERS

Sometimes, birds encounter high mountain ranges across their migration path. Sometimes, the winds that blow in the right direction are high up. To cross mountains or catch winds, birds can reach impressive heights. Migrating birds start off low, then gradually fly higher and higher. The highest flier is the Ruppell's vulture of northern Africa, which has been seen at 37,000 feet (11,300 m).

TERN AGAIN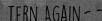

The Arctic Tern makes the greatest migration of all. Late every summer, this small bird heads south from the Arctic. It flies around the world to Antarctica to catch summer there. Four or so months later, it flies all the way back for the Arctic summer. The round trip is an incredible 44,000 miles (70,000 km). On the way north, it flies more than 320 miles (520 km) every day.

NORTHERN PROMISE

Compared to a tern, the northern wheatear is tiny. Yet it, too, makes an astonishingly long journey. It weighs barely 0.8 ounce (25 grams) but it makes a round trip of more than 18,640 miles (30,000 km). Every spring, it flies all the way from the Sahara in Africa to the Arctic, crossing deserts and mountains on the way. This is the greatest journey by any songbird.

Arctic

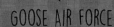

Antarctic

GOOSE AIR FORCE

The migrations of geese are one of the wonders of the natural world. They are all large birds, and they fly together in large flocks. Many fly in a V-formation. This helps the birds stay together and it saves energy as the front birds shelter the birds behind, which is why they take turns flying in front.

THE BEST OF THE BEST

THE CROW FAMILY
SPECIES: 120
LIVE IN: Most places, except for the poles and the tip of South America
EAT: Insects, bugs, worms, and fruit

Known by scientists as corvids, the crow family includes ravens, rooks, jackdaws, jays, and magpies. They are medium to large birds.

SONGBIRDS
SPECIES: 4,000
LIVE IN: Everywhere but the poles
EAT: Mostly seeds, fruits, nectar, insects, small birds, and small lizards

Known by scientists as passerines, or perching birds, songbirds include warblers, sparrows, blackbirds, and robins.

SWIFTS
SPECIES: 100
LIVE IN: Most places but the polar extremes and deserts
EAT: Mostly flying insects

Swifts are among the fastest flying birds of all. Many have a characteristic forked tail and long swept-back wings.

BARN OWLS
SPECIES: 16
LIVE IN: Most places except Antarctica and Micronesia (islands in the western Pacific Ocean)
EAT: Small mammals, such as mice

Barn owls are one of the two families of owls. They have large heads and a characteristically heart-shaped face.

EAGLES
SPECIES: More than 60
LIVE IN: Three-quarters live in Eurasia and Africa
EAT: Small to medium mammals and fish

Eagles are big birds of prey with huge hooked beaks for tearing flesh, strong muscular legs, and powerful talons.

POTOOS AND NIGHTJARS
SPECIES: More than 100
LIVE IN: Most places, except for the far north and south, and the Sahara
EAT: Flying insects

Potoos and nightjars are nocturnal birds that catch flying insects in their gaping mouths.

WEAVERBIRDS
SPECIES: 110
LIVE IN: Southern Africa and India
EAT: Seeds

Weaverbirds all weave elaborate nests. There may be as many as ten billion of one species, the red-billed quelea.

TANAGERS
SPECIES: 240
LIVE IN: Tropical America
EAT: Anything, especially fruit, seeds, nectar, and flowers

The tanagers are a large class of finches. They include the Galapagos island finches known as Darwin's finches, which include woodpecker finches.

LYREBIRDS
SPECIES: 2
LIVE IN: Australia
EAT: Insects, bugs, and worms

Lyrebirds are known for the spectacular tail feathers of the male, and for their amazing skill at mimicry.

TERNS
SPECIES: More than 50
LIVE IN: Everywhere
EAT: Fish

Terns are medium-sized seabirds. They are experts at diving for fish and great fliers, often covering long distances to reach breeding grounds.

SPECIAL SKILLS

As with the animals featured in this book, there are many that have a skill that's so special and so much more amazing than anything humans could do. Just being able to fly, of course, is a special skill that most birds have. But they have others too.

SOARING AND GLIDING

Some birds glide on the air, barely flapping their wings. This saves a lot of energy, and helps them to stay aloft much longer. The best gliders are often large birds, such as the albatross, condor (left), vulture, and eagle, which can glide to scan for prey. Some birds use rising currents of air to soar higher with no effort.

DIVING DEEP

Birds are not only good at flying. Penguins and many other birds are excellent swimmers too. And a number of seabirds are remarkable divers, plunging deep into the sea in pursuit of fish. The deepest diver is Brünnich's guillemot (right). This bird, also known as the thick-billed murre, has been recorded making a dive of 690 feet (210 m).

MIGHTY GRIP

Birds of prey have a remarkably strong grip, and their talons are long and vicious. Those of the harpy eagle (left) crunch together with a force that's nine times as strong as the average human's grip— and quite a lot more crushing than the bite of a wolf or a bear.

CRASH-TESTED

Even the best diver has to be very careful to avoid injury when hitting the water. A gannet (right) smashes into the water much, much faster when diving for fish—with no ill effects. That's because its skull is reinforced like a built-in crash helmet. It also has built-in airbags in its neck and shoulders that can be inflated to cushion the impact. This means it can hit the water so fast—90 miles per hour (145 km/h) or more—that fish are knocked out by the impact.

JUST SWALLOW

The tawny frogmouth (left) doesn't bother to hunt. It just sits perfectly still and waits for dinner to jump into its mouth—which it does. Because the frogmouth is camouflaged to look like a tree stump, small birds, frogs, and lizards venture close without realizing there's any danger. But if they do come too near, the frogmouth opens its gaping mouth, snaps it shut, and swallows the victim whole in a fraction of a second.

INDEX

THE AUTHOR

John Farndon is Royal Literary Fellow at Anglia Ruskin University in Cambridge, United Kingdom, and the author of a huge number of books for adults and children on science, technology, and nature, including international best-sellers. He has been shortlisted four times for the Royal Society's Young People's Book Prize.

THE ILLUSTRATOR

Cristina Portolano was born in Naples, Italy, and studied in Bologna and Paris, graduating in Comics and Illustration. Her artwork has appeared in Italian magazines and comic books such as *Delebile* and *Teiera*. She lives and works in Bologna, and her first book has recently been published by Topipittori.

Picture Credits (abbreviations: t = top; b = bottom; c = center; l = left; r = right)
© www.shutterstock.com:

2 cl, 6 cl, 6 bl, 7 tr, 7 cl, 7 br, 9 tr, 10 bl, 13 tr, 14 bl, 17 bl, 19 cr, 20 br, 21 tr, 22 br, 24 tl, 27 BL, 30 tl, 30 br, 31 tl, 31 cr, 31 bl, 32 cr.